The International Design Library®

THE CHINESE CUT-OUT DESIGN BOOK

Designs from the World of Nature

Ramona Jablonski

PUBLISHERS, INC.
Owings Mills, Maryland

Copyright © 1980 by Ramona Jablonski
All rights reserved

All individual designs in this book may be used in any manner without permission. However, no grouping of 15 or more designs in a single collection for commercial purposes, and no part of the text may be used or reproduced in any manner whatsoever, electrical or mechanical, including xerography, microfilm, recording and photocopying, without written permission, except in the case of brief quotations in critical articles and reviews. The book may not be reproduced as a whole, or in substantial part, without permission in writing from the publishers.

Inquiries should be directed to
Stemmer House Publishers, Inc.
2627 Caves Road
Owings Mills, Maryland 21117

A Barbara Holdridge book
Printed and bound in the United States of America

First printing 1980
Second printing 1983
Third printing 1990
Fourth printing 1999

Introduction

CHIN WU SAT ABSORBED IN HIS WORK, pretending not to hear the soft scuffle of slippers behind him, and the whispered, "Tsst, ssst! Quietly! He'll hear you!" He knew what was going to happen. In the next moment he was engulfed, in a flurry of small arms, soft clothing and giggling voices. "We've got you, Chin Wu! We've got you now!"

"Look, we've brought Spring Flags for your hair!" Small hands were attaching the red and gold ornaments to the thick knot of his hair.

As they stepped back to admire their handiwork, one asked, "What are you doing, Chin Wu, here, all by yourself?"

Without a word, the thin man stood up and spread his arms wide. The long sleeves of his robe fluttered free and made the children gasp with delight. They had cut cheery good-luck symbols from paper to make the flags for his hair. Chin Wu had cut his own Spring Festival wishes out of the sleeves of his robe!*

The adults all thought that Chin Wu was somewhat eccentric. After all, nobody wore flags in his hair anymore. They might be used in decorating the house and the garden sometimes—but certainly not in a man's hair. And to ruin a perfectly good robe like that—was not this a sure sign of mental deficiency?

But the children knew otherwise. They knew that Chin Wu was one of them.

The children always looked forward to Spring Festival time. The adults were so busy cleaning, and bustling about the house, that they were left to entertain themselves. They had seen the old papercutter appear as if by magic in the street. They had stood shyly by and watched him set up his little table, lay out his row of tools and dye-pots with their brushes propped against wire holders. They were fascinated as he carved tightly clamped stacks of plain paper into scenes and shapes that seemed to form like magic before their very eyes.

---
* From an account written by Chow Mi in the thirteenth century.

The papercutter whom Chin Wu's young friends watched was a professional—a "pilgrim of lakes and rivers." He was numbered among those men of no social status who traveled about making and selling their papercuttings for a living, and who often developed an extremely high degree of skill.

Hua yang (embroidery patterns) and funeral products were the mainstay of their income. At holiday time, also, their cuttings were essential in making preparation for the celebrations. They worked in the open where everyone could watch, setting up their tables and equipment wherever there was space—at fairs, in market places or in temple courtyards. Their collections of tools could be modest or elaborate. Some were bought, most were homemade—scissors, knives with blades of sharpened metal strips bound into bamboo handles, punches, gouges, needles. A sharpening stone was close at hand, as were pots of dyes and brushes, and the paper—standard white or the red of joy, congratulations, happiness.

The cutting base was a shallow wooden tray filled to the brim with melted animal fat. The fat was made nearly solid by the addition of powdered charcoal. This made a smooth and resilient cutting base. A broad flat spatula lay ready to scrape and smooth the surface between jobs.

The cutter could proceed in one of several ways. He might follow "the way of the knife" and just cut through his stack of papers, letting his heart and hand and tool tell him the way. Or he might do a brush-and-ink drawing, then cut it out. Or he might use an old favorite cutting as a pattern. He would then dampen it and smooth it on top of the stack, then hold it upside down over a lamp with a paper wick. The heat from the lamp would dry the cutting at the same time the soot was deposited on the paper around it, leaving a negative pattern to work from.

With his pattern prepared, the cutter would dust the surface of his tray with flour to prevent sticking, then put his stack of ten to twenty sheets of paper on top of it. The stack was sewn together with needle and thread, or held with twists of paper inserted through slits in each corner, or else simply tacked to the border of the tray.

With the pattern on top, the cutter set to work with his tools. Knives were usually held upright and pushed vertically down through the stack, then pushed or pulled to make the cut. Usually small shapes were cut first. Each section was removed as it was cut, by piercing and picking it up with a pin. Larger parts of the design were cut next. Finally, the outline was cut with knife or scissors.

If the cuttings were to be colored, the stack would be dampened first, and the dyes applied to the top layer only. Since the paper was unsized, the dye seeped straight down through the stack, coloring each layer as it went. The stack was allowed to dry and the layers separated one by one as a customer came to buy.

Usually, as fast as they could be dried and separated, people bought them up to take home for use in the holiday festivities. The dyed ones were glued on windows, mirrors, walls, doors and any other place that needed brightening. The plain ones were put away to be fastened to gifts or embroidered onto clothing.

The children watching the professional papercutter were also accustomed to seeing their mothers and female relatives work designs in cut paper, using slim, pointed scissors. The most gifted of the women wanted only the thin, smooth-grained paper from Ningkuo in Anwei province for their work. It was this paper, along with scraps of shiny foil, that the children had used to make their gifts for their friend Chin Wu.

By this time in the thirteenth century paper and papercuttings had become a common part of the lives of the Chinese children and their people. It had not always been so. For several centuries after its invention about 105 A.D., paper had belonged only to the rich. The process of making it was lengthy and expensive. The mulberry had to be stripped of its outer bark, because only the strong, thin fibers of the inner covering would do. These fibers were left exposed to the elements to bleach and toughen. They had to be boiled or steamed, and pounded just enough to separate the fibers but not to break them into pieces, as is done in European papermaking. A silk screen was then dipped into the vat and the fibers brought up on it in a tangled mass. Excess pulp and water had to be shaken off—so matted was the fiber that the water could not drain through. Several dippings and shakings later, the screen was covered with a still exquisitely thin and amazingly strong layer of felted fibers that would ultimately become a dry sheet of paper.

When it was all done it was an amazing product! Tough, ideal for brush painting and writing, it was also lightweight, easy to transport and store. It could be folded, molded, stretched (if you were careful and dampened it first), and cut into marvelous shapes.

In short, paper was too miraculous, too useful to remain the province of the few for very long. By the time of the T'ang dynasty (618-906 A.D.), paper had thoroughly permeated Chinese society. Its uses ranged from the frivolous to the industrial. The poet Ts'ui Tao'Yung describes a Spring Festival celebration in which palace gardens were decorated with flags welcoming the season. Guests were given paper flags of red and silver, and noble ladies wore paper butterflies and sparrows in their hair.

Because of the essentially fragile nature of paper, knowledge of many of its early industrial uses has been lost in antiquity. But some uses can be surmised from the evidence that remains.

For instance, the blue-and-white porcelain of everyday village use in the T'ang period was decorated in the glazing stage by using paper cut-out designs. They were dampened, dipped in powdered oxides, then stuck on the pottery piece over the unfired glaze. In the kiln, the paper burned away, but the impression of the design it held remained in the glaze. The method was both cheap and effective.

Patterns for wood carvings were first worked out in cut paper, which was then pasted on the wood block, there to remain until the carver had finished his work. The pattern was then soaked off. Lacquerware was similarly decorated by masking appropriate areas with a paper cut-out stencil. Designs for leather, metalwork and cotton applique were made easier by the use of cut-paper patterns and stencils.

The art of applying decoration to fabric by using paper cut-out stencils predates the T'ang dynasty. And it is probably one of those few crafts in which the means to the end is as highly appreciated as the end-product itself. Chinese and Japanese cut-paper stencils are valued by many collectors today.

This stencil craft was carried to Japan by a Chinese dyer named Someya Yuzen at the end of the seventeenth century. For this reason, the Japanese and Chinese processes for making and using stencils are very similar. Again, fibers from the mulberry tree are favored because of their strength. The paper is made by a careful process. Then the sheets are treated with the juice of just-ripe persimmons, which has been allowed to age until it is sticky. The astringent quality of the juice makes the paper strong as well as water-resistant. To form sheets of different weights, two or three thin layers are stacked with the grain crisscrossing. The sticky juice holds them together. The sheets are then hung in a closed area and smoked above smoldering sawdust. This hardens and seals the persimmon coating.

The stencil cutter then goes to work. He chooses thick sheets for bold designs and thinner ones for more delicate work. He will cut several identical stencils at one time, by fastening a stack of paper on a cutting-board surface. Cutting is done carefully so as not to misalign the sheets. Each stencil must fit exactly on top of the one underneath.

The equipment and work are much like that of the professional papercutter. Punches come in all shapes: crescents, petals, circles, triangles, squares and leaf shapes sometimes make holes so small that they can only be seen when the stencil is held up to the light. All perforations on the stencil must be cut out with a sharp edge. If something like a pin or needle is used to punch a hole, a burr will result which will keep the dye or resist from passing through and making a clean shape on the fabric.

As the cutter comes close to finishing the design, he may stop long enough to lift one sheet carefully and insert a netting of fine silk threads. The netting is secured at the edges with glue. He carefully replaces the top sheet, making sure that it is glued exactly on the one underneath. The result is a stencil of double strength. The silk threads are so fine that they do not interfere with the passage of resist or dye through the openings. The stencils are then put away to harden and strengthen with age. Some will not be used for years. Well-made paper stencils can last through 150 applications of resist.

The dyer buys from the stencil-maker the number of stencils he will need to complete a job. One stencil is placed on top of the undyed cloth. A dye-resistant paste made of rice-flour or bean-flour and lime is brushed on through the openings in the stencil that create the design. Then the stencil is carefully lifted and repositioned, and resist paste is applied again as many times as necessary, until the design covers the length of the cloth.

When the paste is dry, the fabric is dipped into the first dye bath. The dye is absorbed by the fabric everywhere except where coated with the resist. When it is dried, the paste is scraped off, and the design remains in brilliant white against a colored background. That color will be steam-set, and then the process may be repeated with other stencils to apply additions to the pattern. Thick dye may even be brushed on by hand. Any remaining paste is washed away, and the final color is again set by steam.

Embroidery, another fabric-based craft and one of China's great contributions to world art, offers a strong contrast. Whereas stencil-dyed cloth designs are bold and sweeping in feeling, embroidery is small and delicate—more intimate.

The production of silk in China began about three thousand years ago. The tradition of embroidery is almost as old, and in this, too, paper played an important part. Projects could be planned and drawn or cut from paper first. This would then be pasted directly to the base-fabric and the design shaped with wave after wave of shining thread.

There was a time when a young lady's accomplishment at embroidery was judged as critically by her betrothed's family as her cooking ability and personal grooming. Even her skill at papercutting and folding was taken into consideration.

Thus the papercutter's clientele consisted largely of these needleworkers. Thousands of small papercuttings had to be produced to supply the demand for *hua yang,* the small embroidery designs sewn on articles of everyday use: caps, aprons, tobacco pouches, tablecloths, comforters. The designs were sold in pairs to be used on slippers, vests, pockets, sleeves and waistcoats. These small designs convey charming and appropriate wishes for good luck, wealth and other benefits.

We have seen how much Chin Wu's young friends looked forward to and enjoyed Spring Festival time. One of the customs they must have delighted in most was the annual renewal of the "window flowers." In the dry climate of northern China, windowpanes made of paper were the custom until a few decades ago. Instead of glass, damp paper was stretched over lattice frames. As it dried, it shrank, making a smoothly stretched window covering. This had the advantage of allowing the passage of light and a small amount of air into the room. But a primary disadvantage was also the inspiration for an art form that has enthralled, entertained and delighted whole populations for centuries—the shadow puppet theater. When darkness fell and lamps were lit inside homes, the domestic activities there were exposed for everyone to see through the shadows cast upon the paper windowpanes. So along with fresh, clean windowpanes, there went up newly made "window flowers"—papercuttings, richly dyed, and glued to the paper pane. Their presence was not only enchanting to look at but afforded privacy, breaking up the shadows of the activities inside.

In the shadow puppet theater, the characters, the paper pane and the papercutter's craft were all brought together about the time of the Sung dynasty. Characters for a story were first cut from heavy paper, jointed for movement and attached to sticks for manipulation. They were held by the puppeteer between a bright light and a translucent screen. The story was told as the puppets acted for the audience seated in front of the screen.

Eventually the puppets were made of sturdier stuff—skins of sheep, oxen or donkeys. But the influence of papercutting remained. Body segments and clothing were decorated with perforated designs and brightly painted. Buildings and background—all the objects, in fact—were cut with an eye to visual appeal.

As the shadow theater flourished, it shed a reciprocal influence on its parent art, the window flower, and probably on papercuttings used for other purposes too. Spring Festival is a time to look to them all. Happy flowers decorate mirrors, fans and screens; they are attached to gifts; ceilings and door posts are decorated with paper prosperity symbols; luck hangings flutter like lace from door lintels, wishing benevolence on all who enter; and when pasted on lanterns, the paper characters seem to dance by themselves, their form and significance enhanced by the flickering light.

In China, red is the color of life and joy—in fact, everything positive—for noble and peasant alike. White is the universal color of mourning. White paper ribbons tied on willow trees planted near tombs are symbolic of new life and the world to come. They also serve as district markers of the burial site—a warning to anyone who would disturb them, that to do so could yield dire consequences indeed. In times past, it was not only against the law to desecrate burial sites, but in addition, the outlaw could expect revenge from the living family. It was the responsibility of each family to honor and care for the souls of their ancestors through careful maintenance and protection of the burial ground. To have the tombs disturbed or disrupted was a disgrace that demanded retribution.

These traditional responsibilities are celebrated by the faithful each year at the Chung Yang festival. Fresh paper markers may be hung, and paper money sprinkled about, to keep the dead resting in peace. Special Chung Yang cakes are decorated with paper cut-out ornaments and first offered to the spirit of the ancestors before being eaten by their loyal descendants.

For centuries, paper has played a more or less dominant role in Chinese funeral customs. In ancient China, particularly when a rich man died, all of his belongings were buried with him. It was believed that a person would receive an estate in the afterlife equal to the wealth that he took with him to the grave. Everything went: clothing, utensils, money, and sometimes even wives, concubines and retainers. Of course, these underground treasure troves were magnets for robbers. And the burden of protecting them weighed heavily on the descendants.

By the time of the Emperor Ho Ti (89-106 A.D.) some families began to push for a change in the customs. With the invention of paper, some began to solve the problem by burying coins made of paper covered with gold or silver foil in place of the real thing. It was not a practice that was accepted easily, since it was apparent that as paper became commonly available, the "rabble" would be able to participate in the custom too. As usual, practicality overcame snobbery, and eventually it was common for most corpses to be accompanied to the grave by a wealth of paper goods.

Usually the rituals would begin as nearly as possible at the moment of death. Family members would immediately sacrifice paper replicas of a sedan chair and two drivers or a boat to speed the soul on its journey. The corpse would be dressed for burial in a richly decorated paper robe—often much more elaborate than he could ever have afforded in fabric while he was alive. All, or as many as possible, of the goods he owned (or wished to own) during his lifetime were duplicated in paper. Often they were full-sized and three-dimensional. Furniture, utensils, clothing, and in later years even cars and radios, were painted in realistic detail. Often, people and animals were constructed in sections and jointed so that they could move in the breeze. Coin replicas were strung on cords through openings in the center just as was done with the metal coins themselves. As an extra precaution, many coins were pierced with hundreds of tiny needle-holes to take care of any hostile demons that might be lurking about. The belief was that the demons would have to leap through each and every hole before the coin was consumed by the flames, or they would suffer loss of face. Conscientious relatives intended to keep those rascals busy!

As religious practices changed, it became acceptable to burn paper offerings on behalf of the dead. This was usually done in decorative incinerators in a temple courtyard. Sometimes temple porches would be stacked to the eaves with offerings bought and brought by the faithful to await the day of burning.

In fact, the practice became so widespread that there was fear for the ecology of the once-lush land, since so much bark was used for the making of paper, especially for funeral offerings. But the rationale, for many, was persuasive: at last even the poor could look forward to better circumstances in the afterlife, providing their survivors were diligent about burning offerings for them.

It is not surprising that the Chinese were the first to see the practical value of paper in everyday life. They were the first to use disposable clothing and toilet paper. Legal paper money was also their invention. And a groom's family always felt easier if their son's intended had a few cleverly made paper clothes tucked away in her trousseau. They could rest assure that he would be properly looked after should his death precede hers.

Papercutting, of course, has been practiced wherever paper has found its way. But the "look," the "style," of paper cut-outs from China remains essentially robust and peasant-like in style, whereas European papercuttings have a more "professional" quality to them. The reason may lie in the tools and those who had access to them. Even though paper belonged to the rich for centuries in China, the tools for cutting it remained foreign to the upper classes—not a part of their everyday life. When they wanted to write, they used brushes. They had no reason to develop skill in using scissors or a knife that had to be fetched. But cutting-tools *were* a part of everyday life for the workers. They were comfortable using them. And their artwork reflects their own outlook rather than that of the upper classes.

In European and Muslim countries, on the other hand, such tools were a part of life for the wealthy and the learned. Writing was done with a quill that had to be kept sharp. A penknife was always at hand for this. Scissors for trimming the paper were probably in the writing box too. So it is not surprising that these tools were used for leisure activities and hobbies as well, and that the resulting artwork reflects a more "refined" outlook.

Papercutting in modern China has had to make concessions to the times. Because of the tremendous numbers needed for export as well as at home, some quality assurance is necessary. Precut stencils are often used to assure predictable results. But the government is also seeking out and supporting old masters of the craft, so that they can teach and inspire new generations in this age-old art.

R.J.

Sources for Chinese Papercuttings

China Books and Periodicals
East Coast Center
125 Fifth Avenue
New York, New York 10003

Exotic Papercraft
619 Lilac Way
Lombard, Illinois 60148

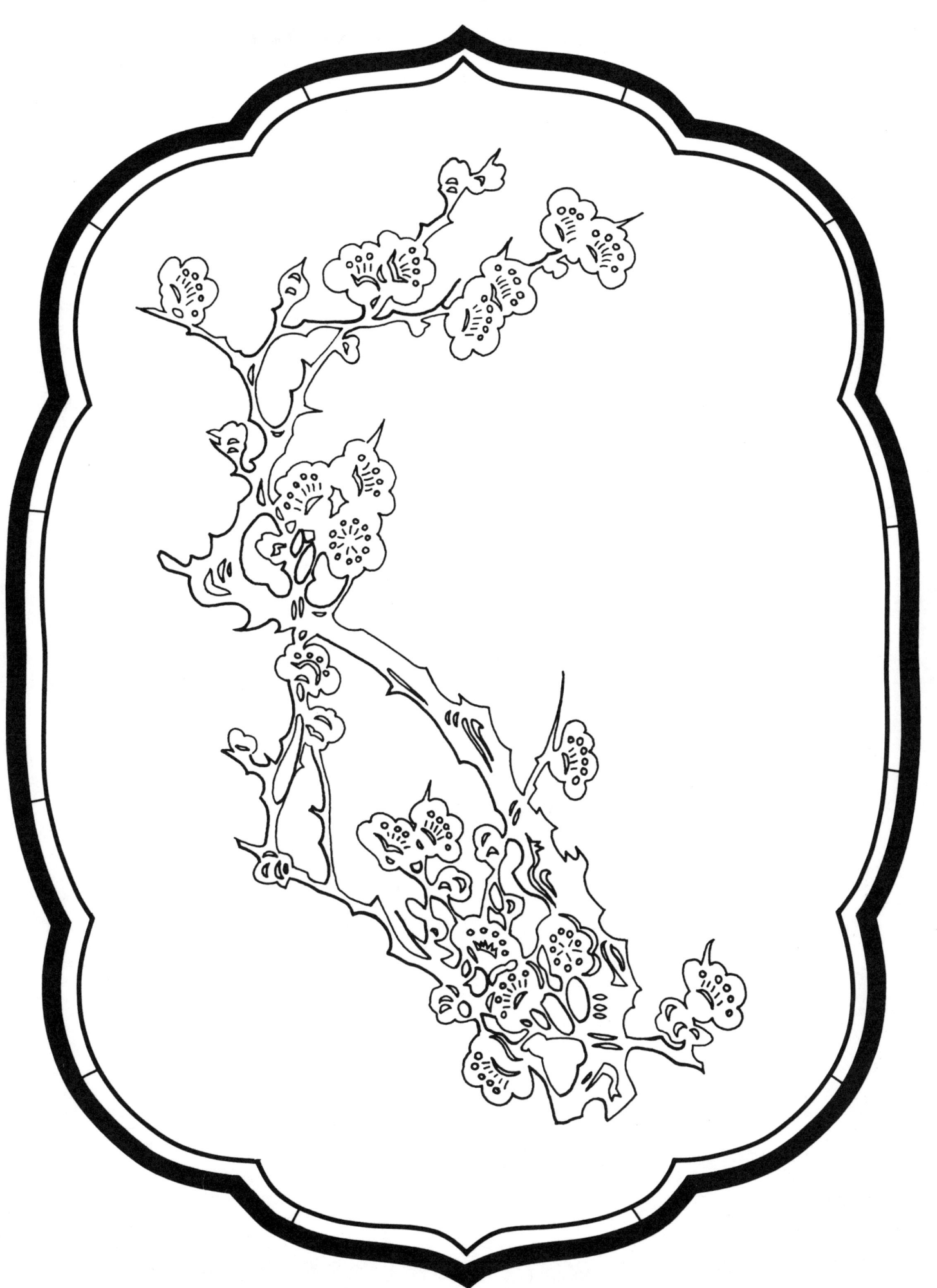

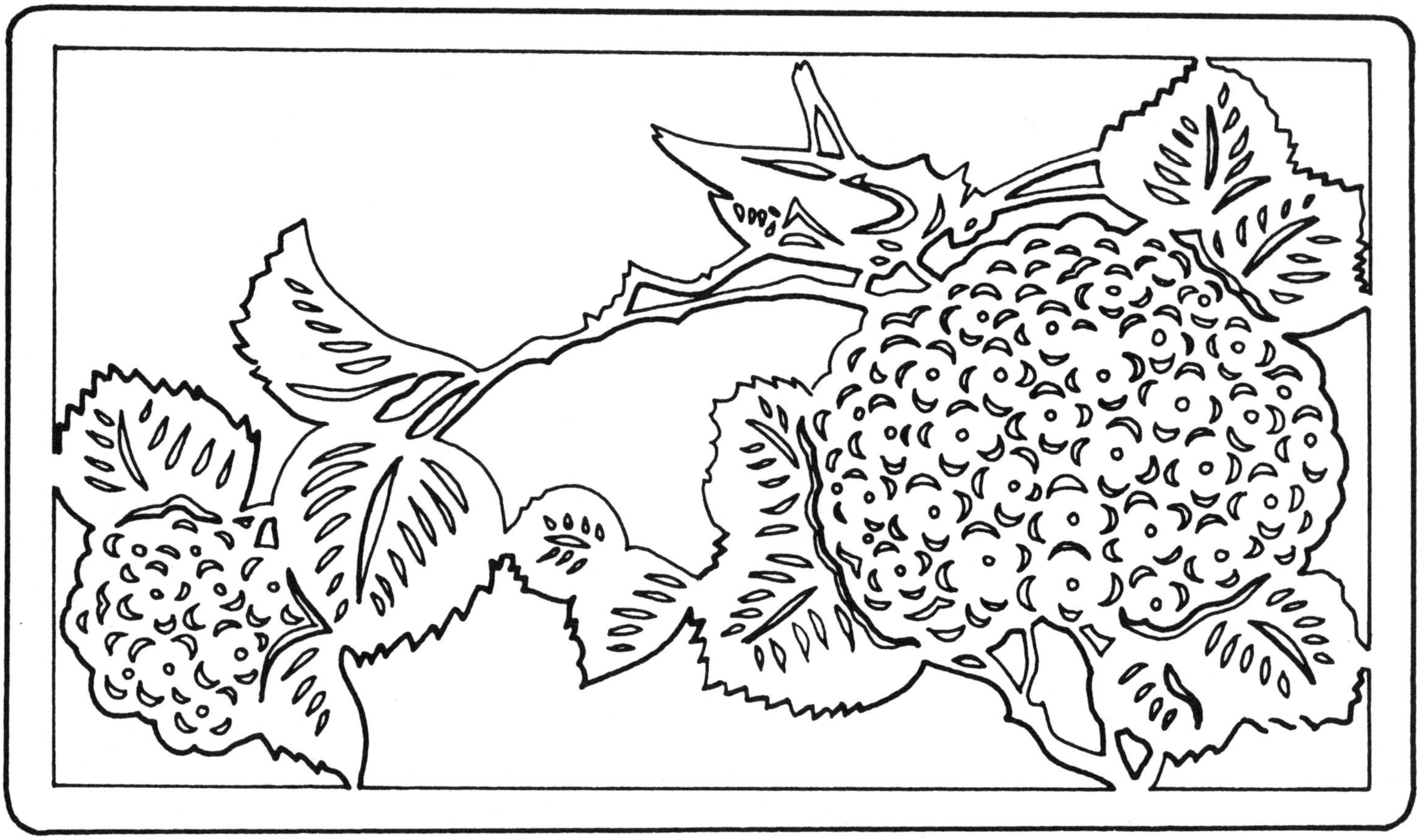

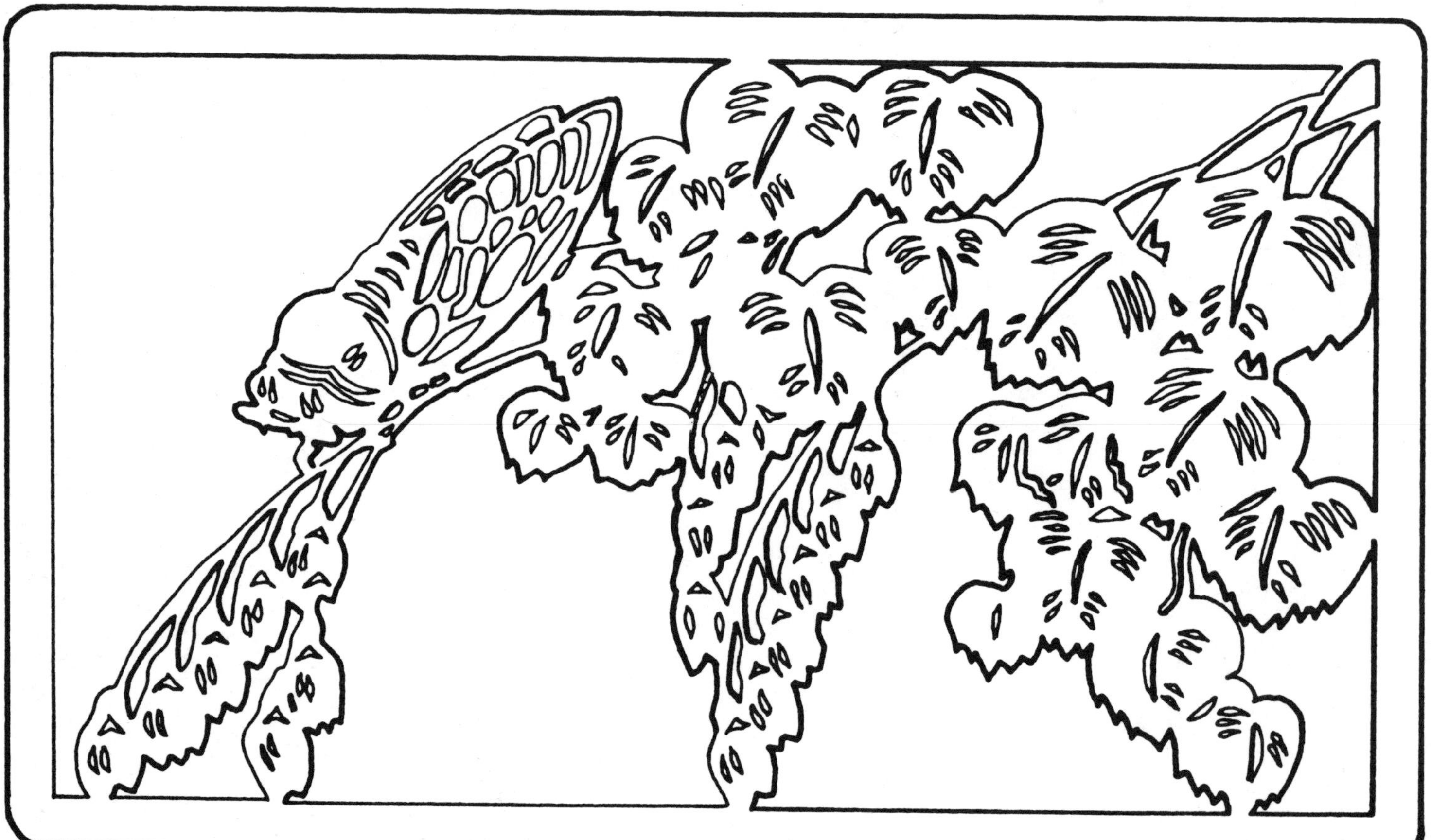

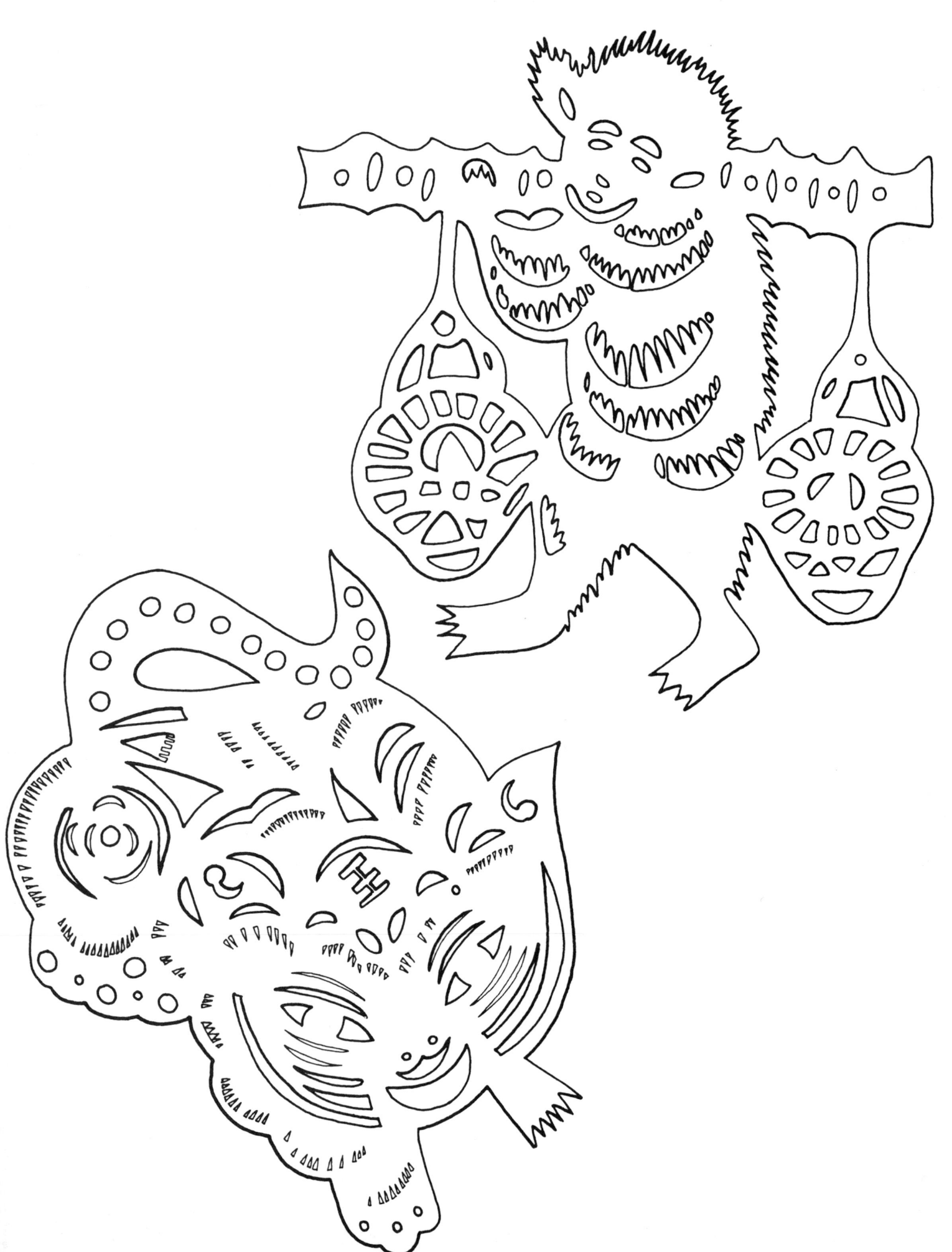

Colophon
Designed by Barbara Holdridge
Composed in Timese Roman with Abbott Old Style display by
 Brown Composition, Sparks, Maryland
Color separations by Capper, Inc., Knoxville, Tennessee
Printed on 75-pound Williamsburg Offset and bound by
 United Graphics, Inc., Mattoon, Illinois